The Homeschool Parents'
**How-To Series**
- Book 2 -

# How to Make Learning MEANINGFUL, MEMORABLE and FUN!

## Lynn Dean
### Creator of Discover Texas

# Foreword

The material for this book, like all the books in the Homeschool Parents' How-To Series, first appeared as a seminar presented at homeschool conventions in my home state of Texas.

Over and over parents responded enthusiastically and asked me to make the material available in book form so they could refer back to the information through the course of their homeschool journey.

I'm happy to do that.

Because the material was designed for presentation in a one-hour workshop setting, these books are short but packed with useable information.

Thanks for this book goes to all the encouragers who helped our family along the way--generous family members who made mind-expanding vacations possible, creative homeschool moms and dads who organized field trips or invited my children to come work alongside them, community leaders who welcomed and patiently trained youth workers. You opened the doors to discovery for my children, and I am grateful!

# Contents

How to Make Learning Meaningful, Memorable, and Fun     1

Learning is More than "School"     5

Teaching From Life     9

    Cooking     11

    Lemonade Stand     15

    Real Life Science     19

       Biology

       Chemistry

       Physics

       Astronomy and Meteorology

    Writing     25

    Socialization     27

The Advantages of Real Life Socialization     31

    A World of Opportunities     31

    Sharing Life with Real People     33

    Building a Heart of Compassion     34

Slice-of-Life Learning Fits All Learning Styles     37

    Life is a Field Trip     38

    Learn by Doing with Unit Studies     41

    Personal Discovery     45

    Biographies, Historical Fiction, and Movies     49

    Family Discussions     53

The Challenge of Discipling Adults     55

    Educate     57

    Instruct     59

    Teach     61

    Train     65

Summary     69

# How to Make Learning
## Meaningful, Memorable and Fun

I have a confession to make. I was (am?) a bit of a nerd.

I loved school. Really. So much so that when I got home from school, I played school after school. I lined my dolls and stuffed animals up in chairs and lectured them. I even tried to make my younger sister sit in a chair while I lectured her.

That didn't work out as well.

As a reward for being a ~~hopeless nerd~~...er...good student, I was allowed to help out in the school library whenever I finished my work early. And oh! What a thrill that was to my book-loving heart! Again...really.

Older, more socialized, and hopefully advanced almost to the status of "geek," I am now willing to admit that my former nerdy behavior was probably less than typical.

Let's be honest. If your grade school teacher assigned a four page report on aquatic life and took you down to the library to find some books to research, would you have felt the thrill of discovery?

Probably not.

But what if you had the opportunity to learn about fish in other ways? What if...

- your dad took you boating on a river or lake one Saturday, fishing rod in hand?
- you took a vacation to the beach, picked up shells, and poked a blade of dune grass at stranded jellyfish and

crabs in their holes?
- you made a trip to an aquarium...or even a trip to the pet store to stock a small aquarium in your room?
- you learned to snorkel or scuba or found one of those places that lets you swim with the dolphins?
- your mom brought whole fish, lobster, or octopus home from the grocery store and let you dissect them?

We can probably agree that any or all of those activities would be more meaningful, more memorable, and more fun than a trip to the library. (Gasp! There...I admitted it.)

Sadly, in traditional school we never even made it to the library for most subjects. Especially once we got past grade school, field trips and hands-on activities were considered a waste of time.

My experience with history was fairly typical. We sat in our hard little chairs at our little brown desks while the teacher read to us from our textbook—names and dates of dead people. I did not know who those people were or why they were important. There weren't even any good pictures—just small, fuzzy ones in black and white. In my mind, those people and the things that happened in their lifetimes were absolutely unrelated to my own life and interests.

Is it any wonder I hated history?

But what if, instead, we'd...
- tasted Native American pemmican,
- built a teepee on the playground,
- lashed together a travois, or
- tried our hand at using an atlatl to throw a dart?

Think of the discussions we might have had about food preservation, low impact housing, early modes of transportation, and tangential velocity!

Instead of just reading about world explorers, what if

we'd made astrolabes out of soda straws taped to paper plates, using our plastic protractors to mark out the degrees and sighting in the North Star? To think that the world was explored by brave men who risked unknown oceans in tiny ships with instruments that were not technologically advanced, yet were elegant in their simplicity! Those are men I might like to read more about.

What if we'd re-enacted segments of history, actually experiencing what it's like to push a bill through Congress or how it might have felt to live in Jamestown, in Plymouth Colony, or through the Civil War?

Closer to home, what if we'd heard from our own parents and grandparents what it was like to live through the Great Depression, a World War, or the Civil Rights era?

When we lecture students about history, we inform them about events that happened to someone else— someone dead and gone whom none of us knew personally. They may listen politely, but it is hard to relate to someone else's story. It happened to them, not to us.

However, when we experience history—or any other subject—for ourselves...when we see it first-hand, hear it, smell it, taste it, and get our hands dirty with it...then the experience becomes our own. As Benjamin Franklin once wrote, "Tell me, and I forget. Teach me, and I remember. Involve me, and I learn."

We understand why a subject is important when we've felt for ourselves the need for new skills. The challenge of our own limitations inspires us to grow and change.

We remember what happened when events become part of our personal experience, because they happened to us!

And when we are actively involved in learning—when we're allowed out of our hard little chairs and away from our little brown desks—learning is more meaningful, more memorable, and also more fun.

Whether we call this type of education discovery learning, immersive learning, real-life or real world learning, it is vital to give our children the adventure of learning as a lifestyle for a lifetime. This book is about how to introduce that excitement into your child's educational experience.

<u>Notes to Self</u>

# Learning is More than "School"

When learning loses appeal, it also loses effectiveness. Learning is so much more than "school"!

**Studies show that we remember only:**

- 5% of what we hear in a lecture
- 10% of what we read
- 20% of an audio-visual presentation
- 30% of a demonstration
- 50% of a group discussion
  **But when learning is ACTIVE—when we...**
- experience something for ourselves,
- enact a simulation or dramatic presentation
- or share with others what we've learned...
  **Retention jumps to 75%-90%!**

Too often we take exciting skills and topics and turn them into boring school courses by processing all the life out of them. We remove them from their environment, isolate and analyze them, chop them into segments we think we can manage in a 30-minute lecture with a follow-on workbook assignment, and present what was once a lively and vibrant topic like so much canned salmon.

Traditional education is, by nature, compartmentalized. It has to be. Large numbers of children are intended (at least ideally) to progress along an assembly line of indoctrination and preparation at a pace similar to peers of their same age. Knowledge is compressed, segmented, and presented in an environment that is completely separate from the real world where students will use that knowledge. Traditional school is a laboratory, if you will. Even the tests administered in traditional schools have little application to the real-life situations that will one day test students' true abilities.

As a result, many students learn in isolation— disconnected from life. They are like children growing up in large cities who have no idea that beef comes from cows, that chickens lay eggs, and that applesauce is made from juicy red apples that grow on trees. They've never seen a farm. They've only seen grocery stores and fast food joints. For them, applesauce comes from plastic containers, eggs come in cartons, and beef comes from McDonald's.

This helps us to understand why so many children whine, "Why do I have to learn this? When will I ever have to know this?" They have not yet experienced the real world where the skills they are learning will become useful. The connections between knowledge and real life are broken.

Learning in isolation from real experience is like trying to enjoy a concert by listening to a poor-quality reproduction of a recording. Whether you listen to it on your old turntable or spend big bucks on the latest digital player, the recording can never equal the live performance—the experience of sitting in the acoustic hall, eyes closed, while the music swirls around you and your heart thrums to the beat of the percussion. If our goal were to inspire a child to love music and to do the hard work of practicing an instrument, which experience is more likely to produce the desired results?

If our goal is to inspire our children to love knowledge and learn eagerly, are we more likely to achieve that goal by introducing them to the real world or by compelling them to study a second-hand imitation from textbooks?

Motivational speaker Les Brown quips that if information alone could change people, we'd all be skinny, rich, and happy. Experience has impact. When we give our children experiences that inspire an memory that has emotions attached, we touch their minds and also their hearts.

Notes to Self

# Teaching From Life

If you homeschool, what first inspired you? I will confess that at the beginning I imagined playing school at home with my children all lined up in little chairs, listening attentively. That fantasy did not last beyond our first week! It was then that I realized what I really wanted to do was show my children the wonders of the amazing world God has created. To do that, we were going to have to get out into that world.

As a result, there was much less "home" in our homeschool.

Yes, we must teach skills incrementally—building one upon the other—but we can still teach in the context of real life.

Instead of stewing that apple until it is no longer recognizable and smashing it into a bland sauce, what if we present it instead in manageable slices? The idea is to give our children "slice of life" discipleship that becomes a sort of apprenticeship for adulthood. I am not saying that we should never use textbooks, but whenever possible we should reinforce the academic skills our children receive from their lessons with experiences in the context of real life.

When we do this, "school" is always in session! That can be a big bonus if you live in a state that requires you to count and report hours of education. Once you learn to see all of life as an educational opportunity, getting in enough teaching time will never be a problem.

Opportunities abound, and many require very little effort. Teaching from real life is mostly a matter of learning how to look for teachable moments.

Let's look at a few examples.

Notes to Self

## COOKING

Something as simple as preparing food can provide any number of teaching opportunities.

Very young children can count with you as you add ingredients. When they're a bit older, shopping can set the stage for real-life mathematical story problems.

I learned this by accident one day when I wanted to make an apple cake. Before we left for the grocery, I sent my youngest to see how many apples were in the refrigerator. Once we reached the produce section, I sent him to select apples, saying, "My recipe calls for a dozen apples. Please go pick out however many we need to make the cake."

"How many should I get?" he asked.

"How many do we have at home?"

"Five." He was sure of that.

"Okay. I need a dozen. Do you know how many a dozen is?" When he shook his head, I explained, "A dozen is twelve. We need twelve apples to make the cake."

"Okay," he said, "so how many should I get?"

"Well if I have five apples and I need twelve, how many more will we need to buy?" After a long pause I asked, "Five plus how many more makes twelve?"

Finally he got it...and, more importantly, I got it. This child was making very good grades on his daily addition and subtraction drills, but he was not yet seeing the connection between the numerals on the page and the number of objects those numerals represent. Memorizing math facts without understanding the connection to real life is absolutely useless...and more common than you might think. No wonder so many children are frustrated with math!

Yet children have an intuitive understanding of math

from a very young age. Try dividing a pizza or a plate of cookies into fractional components, and I guarantee your children can tell you if someone's portion is "greater than" or "less than"!

Whether you're measuring dry and liquid ingredients, working with fractions of cups and teaspoons, or doubling recipes or cutting them in half, it's easy to find ways to teach math while cooking.

But math isn't the only subject you can "cook up". The kitchen is also a great place to teach science. What nutrients do our bodies need to grow healthy? What's the difference between a fruit and a vegetable? What is a calorie? How do yeast and soda cause bread to rise?

You can take your kitchen-based science studies in many directions.

- Making jelly, yogurt, or cheese becomes a practical chemistry lab as we learn about the reactions of pectin, acidophilus, and rennet or vinegar with other ingredients.
- Perhaps your family would enjoy starting a garden to grow your own herbs, fruits, and vegetables.
- Start a compost pile and learn about decomposition.
- Learn how nutrients make their way from the soil into our foods and, in turn, into our bodies. Truly, "we are what we eat"!
- Learn how to save seeds for next year (and learn how some genetically modified organisms are altered so that they will not reproduce from seeds).
- You might experiment with hydroponics (soilless growth mediums) or aquaponics (water-based growth mediums).

You will likely find that fussy eaters are more willing to try foods they have grown or prepared themselves.

As your children acquire skill, you can prepare them for independent living by turning over the meal planning to them for a single meal or up to a week at a time. Give teenagers a budget and let them plan healthy menus. After you've reviewed their plan, put them in charge of shopping, preparation, and clean-up. They'll develop pride and confidence in their self-sufficiency, you'll get a well-deserved break from the kitchen, and their future spouses will thank you!

Notes to Self
<u>Notes to Self</u>

## LEMONADE STAND

A lemonade stand more or less sums up many of the major purposes of education.

We educate our children because we want them to grow up to be ethical in their dealings, resourceful, and self-supporting don't we?

A lemonade stand can teach kids that success is more than just mixing powders and collecting quarters. Frankly, a lemonade stand teaches more lessons through failure than success, but they're having fun while they're failing, right?

Youngsters will tend at first to apply simple math to their beverage venture by adding up their earnings and dividing them between workers at the end of the day. But the practical mathematics of a lemonade stand illustrate beautifully how math skills are important in many aspects of our decision-making.

- How much does it cost to make a gallon of lemonade?
- How many ounces are in a gallon?
- What size cups will you use, and how many cups can you get from that gallon?
- How much do the cups cost?
- What's your break-even cost for each glass?
- What is a reasonable profit?
- When your friends help themselves to "free samples", what happens to your profits?
- If you work all afternoon and your helper only worked one hour, how do you divide the earnings fairly?
- After operating costs, how much did you make for each hour worked?

   The answers to these questions suggest many other business-related questions.
- Do you understand the difference between gross and

net profits?
- Was the business worth your time?
- Are there ways to lower costs or increase prices to improve profitability?

These may sound like heady questions for small entrepreneurs, but are they not exactly the sort of bite-size slice-of-life experiences we're looking for?

Beyond mathematics and business economics, a lemonade stand can introduce principles of management and marketing.
- How do you keep everyone working together without creating hard feelings?
- How many helpers, really, do you need to have fun? To get the job done? To profit?
- Besides lowering operating costs or raising your prices, what can you do to improve the profitability of your business?
- How can you reach a wider market?

These last questions are where we really have an opportunity to talk to our children about business in the real world. There's an old marketing jingle that says, "He who has a thing to sell and goes to whisper down a well is not so apt to win a dollar as he who climbs a tree to holler." While a lemonade stand operated for two hours after school may be a fun way to pass an afternoon, we miss an opportunity to teach valuable lessons if we don't gently encourage our children to experiment further.
- How can you inform potential customers and attract them to your business?
- You know what they say about "location, location, location." Are some better than others?
- Are some seasons, days, or times more profitable than others?

- Are there other services or products you could offer that would broaden your appeal?
- When all is said and done, is there something the people in your social circle need more than they need lemonade and for which they might pay you?

Your own experiences, creativity, aptitudes and risk tolerance will definitely color the business advice and counsel you give your children, but one thing I wanted my children to understand is that work is work. It can and should be enjoyable, but in the end people pay you to do what they cannot do, don't have time to do, or do not wish to do for themselves. This understanding naturally encourages us to make an assessment of our skills and interests and to keep an eye out for opportunities to serve our communities in ways for which they will be pleased to reimburse us.

...and all that can start with a lemonade stand.

Notes to Self

## REAL LIFE SCIENCE

Science is literally everywhere. It's the recipe God used to create the universe. Finding evidence of that to point out to our children is really not difficult, and when we teach them to "open your eyes of wonder," we find that our own eyes open, too.

### Biology

In the first book of this series (*How to Teach the Way Your Child Learns*) I mentioned that some of my kids' biology materials came from our local grocery. Our meat market sells hearts, tongues, brains, liver, kidneys, gizzards, and intestines—all at very low cost. They work well for purposes of inspection, dissection, and discussion.

Nature hikes can provide your family many encounters with a wide variety of plants and animals—even footprints, bones, and fossils. If you don't want your children to drag specimens home, consider taking along cameras or sketchbooks and pencils to record what you see.

Keep pets. When our children were growing up it seemed that we housed a small zoo with fish, hamsters, birds, cats, and dogs. At times it was a lot to keep up with, but I must say that our children learned a great deal by watching animals be born and, sadly, by watching them die. They observed instinctive behaviors and learned to train their pets. They learned to be gentle and to be responsible for the care of creatures who depended on them.

### Chemistry

If science in general is the recipe God used to create the

universe, chemistry is the list of ingredients. Everything that exists was created from just 118 ingredients (or chemical elements) that can be charted in very orderly fashion yet combined and recombined in infinite ways.

I do not mean to imply that I understand chemical science well at all. Usually I tend to avoid doing those things I'm not good at doing, but I will "come clean" where chemistry is concerned because I think it's important to acknowledge that no one is good at everything. There will be subjects your children need that are not your strong suite. What do you do? Find someone who's really good at it! Fortunately Jane Hoffman is very good at chemistry, and her classic series of <u>Backyard Scientist</u> science books are packed with experiments kids can perform using things commonly found around the house. The experiments are safe, easy, and fun. Jane explains exactly how to do each one and what it shows. It's definitely worth the comparably small effort to see the excitement on your kids' faces.

## Physics

Physics is God playing with math. The rules of physics are the play book of the galaxy. I'm not kidding. The principles of physics absolutely surround us! Once you begin to see them, you'll see them everywhere:

- Help your children build a ramp for their toys or skateboards
- Rig up a pulley system for the treehouse
- Play on a see-saw, then discuss levers and fulcrums
- Play the game "Mousetrap" or "Crazy Clock", then design your own whacky devices
- Examine the gear system on your bicycle (wheels and axles)

- Watch a wood-chopping demonstration (wedge)
- Drop objects of various weights and sizes from the treehouse to test gravity
- Use prisms to cast rainbows on your walls
- Observe what happens to the sound when you shorten or tighten the strings of a musical instrument and pluck them
- Count the petals of a chrysanthemum or the scales of a pinecone while explaining the Fibonacci theory
  See? Physics is everywhere!

**Astronomy and Meteorology**

Our children enjoyed setting up wind gauges and rain gauges and keeping weather charts in their early school years. They learned to watch the clouds as predictors of coming changes in the weather. One month they flipped a coin to "predict" whether it would be hotter or colder, wet or dry the next day and compared their random results to the accuracy of the television weatherman. I'm relieved to report that the local meteorologist had a higher rate of success than we got by flipping a coin.

When our daughter was in 2nd grade, we drove out into the country to get a better view of a comet that was visible at the time, and she asked the difference between a comet and a meteor. I had no good answer, so I suggested she write a letter to a man who published a stargazing column in our local paper. (Bonus points if you noticed how I worked in a real-life writing assignment at the same time.) The stargazer was so impressed with her question that he answered in one of his columns, which further fueled my daughter's interest.

Two years later when the stargazer offered classes at a

local park, I called to ask if his course was appropriate for a family with young children. He remembered our daughter and approved, but was not so sure how things would work out with our son in tow. He was only six, and the classes met very late at night. We agreed that I would bring a blanket in case he got sleepy and that we'd "see how things went." Both children enjoyed the course and our daughter seemed to absorb the explanations of star sizes and constellations, though our youngest often fell asleep under the stars. Science class could be worse, right?

One night at home, our daughter was eagerly telling her dad what she'd learned. She showed him all the constellations she knew until she got to the last one. "It's seven stars that look almost like the Big Dipper, but smaller. They are named for seven sisters..." The Greek name stumped her, but a small voice from the back seat supplied it. "It's the Pleiades." He was listening...and learning!

Fast forward fifteen years. Daughter is grown and gone, and youngest son—now a man—is about to leave for college when we drive out into the country one August night to watch the Perseid meteor shower. We turn off all the lights and lay against the warm car hood, just watching. As our eyes adjust to the darkness, we begin to see an abundance of stars not visible in the glare of city lights. Then our son's deep voice begins to sing, "Oh Lord, my God! When I in awesome wonder consider all the worlds Thy hands have made! I see the stars..." We join him, and when we finish, we go back to our silent watching. But this...THIS...is one of my favorite examples of the beauties of real-life science education.

## Notes to Self

## WRITING

Reading, writing, spelling, grammar, punctuation—there's almost nothing more important to your child's future success than a good grounding in these skills. While they're learning, you'll probably have to do some drills, but that doesn't mean you can't spice things up.

Instead of spelling tests, we started each day with a 15-minute spelling bee. Each child took turns spelling words from lists at their own grade-level. The only words they were assigned to write five times were the ones they missed. (Why practice words you already know how to spell?) Talk about an incentive to study the list in advance!

When it comes to practice, having a real reason for writing can make all the difference.

Instead of writing reports, how about writing letters to Grandma, to a pen pal, to someone in a nursing home, or to a soldier overseas?

I assigned our initially-reluctant writers to generate a cartoon each day. The drawings could be simple—stick figures are fine, though you may be amazed at your kids' creativity once the ideas start flowing. The actual writing is short enough to be fun and painless, but the daily exercise teaches consistency, plot development, and dialogue as well as spelling, grammar, and punctuation.

Our local newspaper had a teen editorial staff. As a young teen our daughter enjoyed the opportunity to write about things that were important to her once each month, and the positive feedback she received was very affirming. She went on to minor in journalism and still enjoys writing a blog for her business.

Blogging can be another worthwhile activity. Your teen may need a bit of direction and oversight, but the possibilities for wholesome topics are literally limitless, and the experience may lead to bigger endeavors down the road.

If you have a student who is really enthusiastic about writing, how about letting them try their hand at writing for publication? Many periodicals sponsor writing contests. Some even have special divisions for younger writers. In addition, self-publishing on almost any topic—fiction or non-fiction—has become easier than ever!

For more ideas, my favorite source of inspiration is Marjorie Frank's excellent book *If You're Trying to Teach Kids How to Write, You've Gotta Have This Book!* (Yes, that's really the title.)

Notes to Self

## SOCIALIZATION

"But what about socialization?"

We've all heard it, haven't we—the concern that by homeschooling our children, we're somehow sheltering them from the "real" world? I would submit that the opposite is more likely the case. Where in the real world, outside a traditional school classroom, are you exposed only to people of your same age who live in your neighborhood?

When you teach using slice-of-life discipleship, homeschooling offers an unparalleled opportunity to truly socialize your children by introducing them to a variety of real people participating in real activities in real life.

Here are some ideas for how to do that:

- Your child's favorite sport may provide enjoyable opportunities to practice teamwork skills.
- If you have a home business or cottage industry, let your children observe you at work. When they're old enough, invite them to participate.
- If the company you or your spouse works for embraces "Take our Daughters to Work Day" or "Take our Daughters and Sons to Work Day," participate!
- Ask a variety of professional people of your acquaintance if it might be possible for your child to shadow them for an hour, a day, or a week.
- If your older child shows true interest in a career path, look into arranging an apprenticeship. This could be for a short time, a summer, or for a year or more.
- When they're old enough, let your children get a part-time job. The skills they learn in applying for a position, interviewing, showing up on time, being responsible to a manager, and working with co-workers will teach them lessons they can never learn in any classroom.

- If they have an entrepreneurial bent, let them start their own business.
- Get involved as a family in community service.
- Take your children to visit a nursing home—perhaps with cards or to present a short holiday program.
- Pack Christmas gift boxes or back-to-school supply packs for children in need.
- Does your church pack meals for a local homeless shelter? Sponsor a Backyard Bible Club for children who live in government housing? Help out with Special Olympics? If there's no outreach in place, you might be able to start one!
- Participate as a family in summer missions.

Keep a record of your child's volunteer services. Not only is this a good thing to include on their student transcript, but these activities also teach them to look for opportunities to give back to their community.

Notes to Self

# The Advantages of Real-Life Socialization

Real-life socialization offers many advantages over the artificial "socialization" encountered by most students in a traditional classroom setting.

## A WORLD OF OPPORTUNITIES

"Rich man, poor man, beggar man, thief. Doctor, lawyer, merchant chief!"

Think of all the jobs people do to support themselves— the hobbies and interests they pursue, the challenges they set for themselves. Can you think of anything more inspiring for youngsters who have their whole lives in front of them? They can literally be and do anything!

I have previously confessed that I was a nerdy kid. I made good grades, so when it was my turn to discuss career options with our high school counselor I went into my appointment filled with expectation. The guidance counselor glanced through my folder and said, "You're a very bright girl. What do you think you'd like to be? A teacher, maybe, or a nurse?"

I'd been giving my future a lot of thought and proudly answered that I wanted to be an architect.

I'll never forget her look of surprise.

"Oh, sweetheart! You're a very smart *girl*." She gave the last word emphasis. "Teaching and nursing are both fine professions."

Fortunately I stuck to my dreams and my parents lent me their support. I have enjoyed designing and remodeling homes for more than three decades, and along the way I've found many other interests that add richness to life.

Who said there could only be one career per person? When your children have the opportunity to interact with people from a variety of professions, they'll learn that many people make career changes as they grow professionally, as their interests change, or as times change. Flexibility is a great quality to develop.

The old gender limitations may also begin to blur. Why can a woman not become an architect, a scientist, a military officer, or a farmer? Why can a man not become a chef, a musician, a dancer, or an teacher? At the same time, don't be surprised if your children find creative ways to stay true to their traditional values. A woman can be a business owner and a devoted mother if, for example, she works from home or schedules her time creatively. A man can provide for his family and still be available to coach a youth sports team or stay involved in his children's lives. Observing how a variety of people balance their work with the other areas of their lives will help your children make realistic choices based on their personal priorities.

And what about those not-so-common passions? Is there a way to make a living by fishing or playing sports or writing stories or building tree houses? Where there's a will, there's a way! Your children's horizons will expand as they meet a variety of people and experience the unlimited expanse of human creativity and potential.

## SHARING LIFE WITH REAL PEOPLE

When young people live in the context of a larger community, they have opportunities to absorb certain truths:

- Nobody has a perfect job.
- Nobody has a perfect life.
- Even heroes have faults.
- Villains have a human side.

Sharing life with real people helps us shed naive idealism and gain a more balanced view of the good and the bad in professions and in people. We learn what we have in common and how we are unique. We encounter new ideas and find our place in the world.

As we rub shoulders with the good, the bad, and the ugly, we begin to understand that "hurt people hurt people." We begin to see, by contrast, that people who feel secure live confidently and show respect for others.

When children share life with a broad spectrum of real people, they learn to interact with people from all walks of life—old and young, rich and poor, brilliant and challenged. They acquire the ability to converse respectfully with everyone, not just those who happen to align with their demographics and personal preferences.

As our children share life with real people, they learn to know their own worth; and when they know their own worth, they can speak graciously with kings without fear.

## BUILDING A HEART OF COMPASSION

When I was a young single woman, my father wisely advised me to observe how a young man treated waitresses and janitors. If he treated them rudely or brushed them off as if they were beneath him, who's to say he would not do the same to me once he no longer needed to impress me? But if he thanked them for their service, tipped well, and tried to make their jobs easier, he was showing a grateful and generous heart.

Kindness and compassion are character traits we'd like our children to develop. There is nothing more likely to teach us compassion for others than walking with them for a while. As we come to understand what their life is like, we learn how to help them and meet their needs with respect.

When our children visit someone who is old or sick, they have the opportunity to notice how difficult it can be to accomplish even simple things and how the hours drag when you're alone.

When our children work with people with special needs, they gain an appreciation for the extra effort they put in, making even small accomplishments a cause for celebration.

When we minister to people who are in need, it's best to go ourselves rather than just sending money across town through channels. Assistance received from an impersonal agency often strips a person of self-esteem, but a sacrificial gift given personally blesses individuals with the dignity of knowing that someone else sees and cares for them. They are no longer invisible and untouchable. Instead, they are loved.

These character traits can only be learned when we step outside ourselves and our own interests to go where the needs are. To raise socially conscious children with kind and compassionate hearts, we must take them with us when we go.

Notes to Self

personal associations—both with their ancestor and the personal experience of our outing—and what was a simple study of cotton as a natural resource broadened into a mini history lesson on the Great Depression as well as a social studies lesson on the Constitutional limitations of government.)

Once we arrived at the cotton gin, the children watched as the big trucks loaded with cotton bolls came in from the field. They watched the big gin remove the seeds and "cotton trash"—the bits and pieces of bolls and stems. (More history as one child shared what he'd learned about Eli Whitney, inventor of the first cotton gin.) The cotton trash was set aside to make compost. (Environmental Science) The seeds were sorted: some to feed livestock, and some to sell for next year's crops. (Business) The gin owner cautioned the students not to eat cotton seeds themselves. The seeds contain a toxic compound called gossypol, but cattle have four stomachs that filter out the poison. (Chemistry; Biology) The kids covered their ears as a big vacuum sucked the cleaned cotton through a flash dryer to remove moisture so the fibers would not rot. They stretched out their hands and felt the heat. They watched the compressor squeeze the cotton into bales, wrap, tie, and label them. (Engineering) Then (under close supervision) they had a few minutes to slide down a mound of cotton seeds. (Just fun, though there were plenty of "Health and Safety" warnings.)

(Pause again to notice how many school subjects we've touched on in a meaningful way and how they're all woven together in the rich fabric of a personal experience with sights, sounds, smells, tastes, and textures to make them memorable.)

Already we'd had a great learning experience, but on the

## Slice-of-Life Learning Fits All Learning Styles

In the first book of this series, *How to Teach the Way Your Child Learns*, we discussed the three different learning styles: visual, auditory, and kinetic.

When children learn actively and in the context of real life, they are free to focus on the aspects of their experience that have the greatest impact.

In real life, the sights, sounds, smells, tastes, and textures blend naturally and reinforce one another. The best and most memorable parts of each experience are built in!

Let's look at some ways to create multisensory learning activities.

## LIFE IS A FIELD TRIP

If you've ever worked in a cubicle, you may have experienced the feeling of emerging into the outside world at the end of a long day. Many times I have emerged from a windowless office and been shocked by the warmth of a summer sun or surprised to realize that it rained or thought sadly, "This was a beautiful, crisp autumn day...and I missed it."

My school had no windows, either. I think maybe that sad aspect of its design was supposed to protect students from drive-by shootings, conserve energy, and eliminate distractions. Unfortunately, it also trained us to live our lives within a very confined space while the world passed by without our knowing much about it.

When we homeschool, we do not have those constraints.

We live in the middle of a field trip. Go!

Less "home"; more "school". Maybe we'd do well to think of education as "world schooling".

Pack up the kiddies and take them with you as you go about your grown-up life. How else will they learn what adults do and how adults act? I've always said I had no interest in raising children. Goodness knows the world has plenty of chronologically advanced people who behave like children. My goal was to raise adults! To that end, I took my children many places.

- They went with me into the voting booth. I impressed upon them what a great privilege it is to be able to choose our leaders, and from the frequency and regularity of such excursions, they knew that voting was a priority to me.
- They went with me when we delivered food to the

housing project across town. They played with the children who lived there, and they learned that most humans hope for pretty much the same things.

- They went to work with me. (That's easier when you run your own business, as I do.) Our daughter rode in a tummy carrier to visit construction sites when she was six weeks old. Our son helped carry and hook up computer equipment at sales conventions, and both of them developed public relations skills in my booth.

A field trip does not have to be spectacular or even particularly entertaining to be meaningful. I suppose one of life's larger lessons is that happiness does not require that we be free to go wherever we want so much as that we learn to want to be wherever we are. As kids we may have complained that there was nothing to do in our hometown, but it was not true. Your kids need never voice that complaint. There is something interesting to see and do just about anywhere you go if you learn how to look for it.

Wherever you are, I guarantee you are surrounded by many highly entertaining field trip possibilities as well. Many of them are free or surprisingly affordable. Sites of interest, historical sites, museums, zoos, art galleries, concert halls, state and national parks, lakes, rivers, caverns...all lie within driving distance.

The possibilities are endless! And as you visit these places, your children will be immersed in sights, sounds, smells, tastes, and textures that will add context to their studies and scope to their lives.

## Notes to Self

## LEARN BY DOING WITH UNIT STUDIES

A unit study is, basically, an interdisciplinary learning activity planned around some particular theme.

Some homeschoolers teach all their subjects—language, math, science, art, history—within the context of a grand exploration of some passionate pursuit. That's certainly one way of doing it, and the results can be richly fulfilling, but if you're not up for an immersive challenge you can still enliven and enhance any subject by including hands-on activities. Even if you're more comfortable using a fairly standard textbook/workbook approach, the addition of unit study projects will place your curriculum in a real-world context and create a "memory hook" of personal experience on which students can "hang" the facts they've learned.

Unit studies don't have to be elaborate or take a lot of planning.

While we studied our state's natural resources, we joined a group field trip to a local cotton gin. As we drove to the gin, I told my kids about their great-grandfather who used to have a thriving cotton gin in the same area. They asked if we could see it, and I explained that it no longer existed. The government compelled some cotton gins to close in order to preserve others during the Great Depression. A lively conversation ensued as our children formed  an emotional link with a relative they'd never met and began to passionately discuss whether governments have the Constitutional right to close the private businesses citizens.

(Let's pause here and point out how our textbook study of natural resources was enhanced by a slice-of-life field trip to a functioning cotton gin. The field trip began to morph into a unit study as our conversation formed the "hook" of

way home we passed a cotton field where a friend was harvesting. He let my son ride with him on the cotton picker—sweeping eight rows down and eight rows back—while my daughter and I gathered wind-blown bolls along the edge of the field. The cotton in just those sixteen rows filled the enormous basket on the picker.

The rest of the way home, the kids were quiet, picking their bolls clean by hand. We talked about how tedious it would be to pick and clean cotton by hand as the slaves did. (History) I shared their grandfather's theory that "picking cotton causes baldness" because all the boys he'd picked cotton with growing up were now baldheaded old men, and we talked about the difference in working hard on your own land for your family's survival and working hard on someone else's land where you never share in the wealth. (Ethics)

Back home, I showed the children how to twist the cotton fibers with their fingers to make yarn. They each finger-spun one boll while I got supper on, then I crocheted one boll into a 2" x 3" sample square. (Homemaking) Looking at the tiny patch, we tried to imagine how many blankets—or sheets, or towels, or blue jeans, or t-shirts, or socks—might be made from the cotton in one field and sold anywhere in the world. (Economics) When we were done, we had a much fuller grasp of the importance of cotton as a natural resource.

This is just one example of how even an impromptu unit study can make learning meaningful, memorable, and fun.

Notes to Self

## PERSONAL DISCOVERY

In my early days of teaching, I was privileged to hear Gregg Harris speak about Delight Directed Homeschooling, a method that uses a child's natural interests and aptitudes to facilitate learning. (Ideas on how to discern your child's natural interests and aptitudes are the subject of *How to Teach the Way Your Child Learns*, Book 1 in the <u>Homeschool Parents' How-to Series</u>.) This method does not advocate leaving a child free to do only what they want, but does point out the advantages of giving your child time and space to explore their interests with a bit of direction and structure from you.

- Does your child have a particular interest in history? See if there are historical re-enactment groups in your area.
- Do you have a budding artist or musician? I'll bet there's someone near you who teaches art or gives music lessons.
- Aspiring actor? Many communities have civic or children's theaters.
- Young athlete? Sports teams abound!
- Promising politician or a heart for social justice? Try Toastmasters or help them volunteer with a cause that aligns with their interests.

Some people are born knowing what they want to do when they grow up. Others may try out several interests before they find one that fits them well. If your child's interests are a little nebulous, that's more than fine. You can still give them time to explore and discover where their skills and interests lie.

Here the computer is a great ally. A search of almost any topic will lead you to quality articles and instructive videos by others who share the interest. Name the interest niche, and you can find others who are interested! This ties in with our earlier discussion of socializing with a wide variety of people from many walks of life. Of course this is one example of the need for direction and structure from you, but with appropriate guidance and oversight your child can reach far beyond the limitations of their current skill level and geographic location to form associations with others who love what they love.

Over nearly three decades of teaching, I've seen students eagerly pursue an amazing array of interests that played an important part in their future.

- One young lady had an interest in longhorn cattle breeding. Though she lived in a city, she participated in 4-H projects and wrote a research paper on how longhorns had been brought back from near extinction by the careful cross-breeding of five distinct lines. She presented her paper in competition, where it attracted attention and was published in a magazine for cattlemen. A few ranchers were impressed and offered her free calves culled from their herds. Her family bought land, she began to build a herd of her own, and eventually became a veterinarian.
- Another young lady had an interest in theater and anime that led her into costume design. She is well on her way to becoming a gifted seamstress.
- One boy took to computers naturally as a very young child. As he got older his father helped him build his own machines, and he took college programming courses while still in high school. From this base, he taught himself almost two dozen coding and scripting languages using online tutorials. He now has a career in internet security, identifying and analyzing malware and devising countermeasures.

- One young man had an interest in classic movies. Through personal discovery, he learned what makes movies memorable, honed his writing skills, and launched an award-winning blog where he posts reviews of movies old and new.
- Two brothers followed their interests with encouragement from parents who made it possible for them to attend annual conferences for independent film-makers. Just out of high school they launched a video production company that has become their livelihood and opened the doors for them to contribute to nationally recognized Christian films while still in their twenties.

Instead of viewing our children's "extracurricular" interests as distractions and wrestling them back into little brown desks piled high with workbooks, is it not often better to harness those interests, keep hold of the reins, and enjoy the ride to see where it takes us?

Notes to Self

## BIOGRAPHIES, HISTORICAL FICTION, AND MOVIES

Strictly speaking biographies, movies, and quality historical fiction are not slices of real life. They are fiction, and fiction, by definition, is not real life. When skillfully handled, however, they can help students relate to subjects vividly even if it's in a second-hand way.

A child who reads about *Johnny Tremain*, for example, cannot help but gain insight into life in America at the time of the Revolution. Very young readers can relate to girls their own age in the American Girls series, and Laura Ingalls Wilder's Little House series is based on her own experiences on the American frontier.

Our family enjoyed watching *Hans Brinker and the Silver Skates* as a holiday treat. Of course, we made a mini-unit study out of it by reading the book first and writing a compare-and-contrast essay about which version we enjoyed more, but both the book and the movie present a delightful glimpse of life in the Netherlands.

Consider travel videos as a way to enhance your study of geography.

Scan the listings of the History Channel or PBS for documentaries that might be appropriate. Did you know that you can stream many of their archived episodes online or as YouTube videos?

While these resources are fictional, we should not discount their value as supplements that can bring subjects to life.

We also should recognize them as stepping stones to real-life accounts—autobiographies, letters, diaries, essays, and interviews, for example.

Even very young children, after reading a book or seeing a movie set in history, would enjoy hearing a grandparent's first-hand recollection of the event and of what life was like for children long ago.

I remember the thrill of discovering a letter my great-great-grandfather wrote home from the Civil War. As he described sleeping in the snow and asked if his mother might find time to knit him some socks and mittens, I could almost hear his voice in those handwritten words. I literally shivered with sympathy.

Whether through fiction, non-fiction, or original sources, the point is that our children learn to view history as more than just "a bunch of dead guys" and that the world beyond their daily lives becomes real to them. When they study people of the past or in other places, we want them to empathize—to put themselves in a place of understanding—and ask

- What do they want?
- Why do they want it?
- What do they believe?
- What will it cost them?

These are the insights that make struggles and achievements meaningful.

## Notes to Self

## FAMILY DISCUSSIONS

One of the most important means of real-life teaching and learning is through communication. TALK to your children. LISTEN to them.

It's scriptural.

In Deuteronomy 6:6-7 God says, "These commandments that I give you today are to be on your hearts. Impress them on your children. Talk about them when you sit at home and when you walk along the road, when you lie down and when you get up."

In any relay race, the critical moment occurs when one runner passes the baton to the next runner. It does not matter how fast the first runner ran if he fails to pass the baton to the next in line. We place the baton of our family values firmly into our children's hands through open communication—by talking to them about the things that matter to us.

Family discussions also help you gauge your student's level of understanding. In a traditional school setting, teachers depend on tests to tell them what percentage of knowledge a child has mastered, but in a smaller setting we can get a much clearer picture by listening to children as they explain what they've learned. We can focus in on exactly what is unclear, and sometimes our children may surprise and delight us with their unique perspective and insight.

Conversation also helps students examine and understand events within the context of their family's worldview. Whether we are discussing the news headlines or casually sharing the day's events, conversation helps children make sense of their world.

Family discussions can also help us establish the

principle that choices have consequences. I'm not necessarily talking about scolding or criticizing when I say that because discussions can help us analyze the possible consequences of our choices before the choice is made. My first career was home design. At the beginning of any new project, I met with the family to hear what they wanted, what they hoped their finished home would look like and how it would function. Then we drew a preliminary plan. The first plan was almost never perfect, but it gave us something to analyze—something to improve. Finally we arrived at a version that provided the best possible end product. A family discussion can do much the same thing by providing a safe place to discuss options. In the larger scope, we teach our children to live deliberately.

Notes to Self

## The Challenge of Discipling Adults

Homeschooling is a growing trend in America. Thousand of parents are pulling their children out of traditional schools and wondering, "Now, how do we do school at home?"

...and that's the wrong question.

The right questions are "How do I disciple my child to become a responsible, happy, successful adult?" and "How do I get my kids excited about learning?"

Children need cheerleaders. They're not quite confident that they can really "make it"—that they can successfully grow to become independent adults. Part of our role as parents is to serve as encouragers and motivators as we lead them from here to there.

It may be true that "you can lead a horse to water, but you can't make him drink," but there are ways of creating a thirst in the horse! Children can get excited about real-life learning because it is relevant and adventurous.

Educating our children is so much more than buying curriculum, assigning lessons, and grading tests. In fact, are those not the very things that made many of us dislike learning? Be honest. Do you have vivid memories of anything you learned out of a textbook? Haven't you learned far more from real life? If you're like me, I'll bet real life has been your best teacher to this day.

"School" does not equal "education." Real education is

the adventure of learning as a lifestyle for a lifetime. That's important, because we live in a fast-changing world. As motivational speaker Les Brown says, "You've got to run fast just to stand still." Our daunting challenge is to prepare our children to thrive in a world we have not seen.

If the goal of education is to disciple adults—to prepare our children for maturity and independence—then we should stop thinking of education in terms of "school". There are many other words that come much closer to describing what it is we mean to accomplish.

## EDUCATE

(from the Latin *educere*, to lead forth)
to develop mentally and morally;
to persuade

Education means leading our children into the adventure of learning. How do we do that?

By giving them someone to follow.

By allowing them to accompany us on ever-expanding hikes along the paths of real life.

Like mother ducks, there is a season for nurturing our young ones in safety, but there is also a time for leading them out into the world—out of the nest, across the grassy bank, and to the water's edge. The mother duck goes in first and calls to the ducklings to follow. Some hesitate, cautious. Others tumble in without regard for risk or danger. Before long, they are all strong enough to swim against the current.

Swimming against the current—developing moral integrity—is as important as developing mentally. I would submit that integrity is *more* important than academic achievement. Strangely, developing the ability to swim strong in all kinds of water is a pretty good definition of what it means to be truly socialized. In school we are taught to stay in line, follow directions, and do what we're told. Unfortunately, many young people are also conditioned not to break rank against peer pressure, not to question the prevailing ideas of the majority, and not to trust their own hearts and do what is right.

When we spend considerable amounts of time living life with our children, we encounter wonderful opportunities to persuade them of the skills and values we consider important.

## Notes to Self

## **INSTRUCT**

(from the Latin *instructus*, *in-* + *struere*, to build)
to provide with authoritative information or advice

When we instruct our children, we offer them a voice of experience.

I've always believed it's best to be honest with children about the challenges we have encountered in the adult world. They may not need the whole truth all at once, but they will face many of the same challenges, and perhaps they can learn from our mistakes. Few of us enjoy being "preached at," but advice is much easier to take when offered humbly, as one who has walked the same road and learned where the rough places are. By instructing our children about the realities they will face, we literally build in wisdom.

Notes to Self

## TEACH

(from the Middle English *techen*, to show)
to guide by precept, example, or experience

    Most parents long to spare their children unnecessary hardship in life. What better way is there to do that than to guide them gently, consistently, and progressively by precept, example, and experience?
    Very often we are teaching when we don't know we're teaching.
    I once offered to teach a friend how to start a business, and we planned to include our children in the start-up so that they could learn from the experience, too. Three months in, my friend had a change of heart, and I was left with the half-finished project. Thus began one of the most difficult years of my life.
    Because we had sold advanced subscriptions to finance the project, I researched and wrote frantically to stay ahead of schedule but eventually fell behind despite my best efforts. I wrote our customers, offering them a refund. One lady begged me to keep the money. She believed in the project and wanted me to continue. My children shouldered a great deal of initiative and responsibility that year, doing their schoolwork with minimal oversight. They also ate a lot of frozen pizza while I plowed doggedly ahead.
    My conscience flogged me. Here I was writing about how to teach through learning adventures, and my own children had to revert to textbooks because I had no time to devote to the very practice I was preaching.
    Finally the project was finished. Only my 10-year-old son was home at the time, but I called him in to celebrate "the last word of the last sentence on the last page."

He cocked his head. "You mean it's over?" (Meaning, I suppose, the whole excruciating ordeal.)

I nodded.

"Mama, why did you do that to us?"

His question wasn't meant to be rude or accusative, but my heart broke. He didn't need to know all the ins and outs of why my friend did not continue, but I could tell him the truth about how I had taken money in advance, how I owed it to customers to deliver the product they had paid for, and about the lady who begged me to continue.

He was silent for a minute, taking in what I said. Then he asked, "Do you mean you did all this to keep your word to one lady?"

"I guess I did," I said, and I wondered if he would understand.

All he said was, "Wow." He understood, and he has grown to be a man of integrity who thinks about how his actions will affect others and swears to his own hurt. (Psalm 15:1-4)

I cried many tears over that project, but it has been a blessing to many people in many ways. Without all of that, though, if God's only purpose for having me do it was to teach my son by precept and example what it means to do business with integrity, then I'd say the experience was well worth the cost.

## Notes to Self

## TRAIN

(akin to the Latin *trahere*, to draw)
to direct growth by pruning, bending, or tying;
to make fit;
to prepare;
to aim

The Biblical admonishment to train up a child in the way
he should go (Proverbs 22:6) is rich in meaning. We are to
prepare our children well and make them fit to do the work
for which God created them. (Ephesians 2:10)

The Bible often uses the metaphor of a fruit tree to
describe an abundant and faithful life full of godly works. In
John 15 Jesus cautioned His followers to abide in Him,
explaining that He is the vine, and that our heavenly Father
is like a vinedresser who takes away any branch that does
not bear fruit and prunes every healthy branch to become
even more fruitful.

Maybe the Germans got it right when they described
kindergarten as a garden of children. Part of our
responsibility as parents is to direct the growth of our
children, gently pruning away childish behavior and foolish
habits. We bend them toward God so that they grow in
healthy directions. I certainly would not advise tying the
little tykes up (no matter how rowdy they get), but I did
learn an important lesson from a gardener who came to
plant a peach tree in our yard.

After he had planted the young tree firmly in good soil,
he took out his pocketknife and cut the branches back so
severely I thought surely he would harm the tree. But he
explained that for the first few years the little tree didn't
need to put its energy into bearing fruit. Instead, it needed

to develop good roots.

Perhaps you've noticed the compulsion of some well-meaning parents to sign their children up for any and every activity—sports, gymnastics, dance—from a very early age. Government schools that once began with first grade at age six gradually added half-day then full-day kindergarten and now offer prekindergarten preparation for children as young as three. Could it be that we are pressuring children to produce fruit too soon? If we took a lesson from the gardener, we might cut back on some of those activities and instead allow our children to become deeply rooted in home and family. With a healthy, supportive root system the tree will be better equipped to bear good fruit when the season is right.

After he'd trimmed the peach tree, the gardener staked and tied it with soft ropes. "These ties will support the tree and help it grow straight even when the winds blow against it, but as the tree grows you should loosen the ties so they don't chafe against the tree's trunk. In about three years, take them off entirely. Otherwise the tree will depend on the ropes to keep it upright, and it won't develop any strength in its own trunk."

Some parents are so enchanted with their little ones that they can't bring themselves to enforce the boundaries of good discipline, but children need boundaries until they are old  enough to make wise choices on their own.

These same parents often experience a growing sense of anxiety as their children grow, and their worries can become full-blown panic when the child becomes a teenager. They respond by tightening the ropes, but discipline applied suddenly at that age only chafes at their strapping saplings. Even if they could succeed in sheltering their children from all winds or coercing appropriate behavior, the child has had no opportunity to gradually develop a core of personal strength. I would far rather the "ropes" come off while the child is still at home to make their youthful mistakes under loving supervision. If their first experience with independence does not occur until they leave home, it can be a very overwhelming experience!

The final word picture associated with training children is that of aiming an arrow. Psalm 127:4 says that children are like arrows in the hand of a warrior. We shape a strong, straight shaft and chip away the rough edges to sharpen them to a fine point. Then we point them in the right direction and launch them with all our might into a world that is far beyond us.

And oh, when they succeed, what a joy it is to watch them fly!

Notes to Self

# Summary

Discovery learning allows our children to sample real life, one slice at a time. We could take a group of students of various ages, aptitudes, and interests out into the world, and each would return with different observations and insights, but in each case the knowledge gained would be uniquely appropriate to the child as an individual.

That's because slice-of-life learning takes advantage of the child's natural interests. They will notice what is new and exciting to them, and they will delight in sharing their insights with you. Is that not much easier than deciding what lessons they are scheduled to learn today and attempting to convince them to be interested?

What a child learns from real life experiences belongs to them. They own the experience, and they will learn to enjoy taking the initiative to learn on their own.

The lessons we learn from experience are deeply personal. We naturally remember the things that happen to us and all the feelings and lessons associated with the experience. Our own memories and experiences are more vivid to us than the things someone else has learned from experiences we cannot relate to.

Children love to share their experiences and what they have learned. From the responses of others they gauge a sense of their own value and develop confidence and self-esteem.

They also develop a sense of their own uniqueness. In sampling many experiences they not only discover their gifts, but also develop a sincere appreciation for the interests and skills of others.

Our children are our students not only in school but in life. They are our most intimate disciples, given to us by God, to Whom we will give account for the way we steward the treasures He has entrusted to us. And long after they are our students, they will continue to be our friends and fellow travelers in God's adventure.

# Other Books in this Series

## How to Teach the Way Your Child Learns!
(Book 1 - ebook and paperback available on Amazon)

## How to Encourage Creativity in Your Child
(Book 3 - ebook and paperback available on Amazon)

## How to Raise a Hero
(Book 4 - ebook and paperback available on Amazon)

## The Homeschool Parents' How-To Handbook
All four titles in ebook and paperback available on Amazon

# Other Educational Works by this Author

## Discover Texas

A hands-on, unit study-based history program to help families discover Texas, one adventure after another!

# Other Books by this Author

## More Precious Than Gold

The bullet that killed Eliza Gentry's fiancé shattered her dreams as well. Clinging to her battered faith, she heads west to escape her grief and runs headlong into the man who caused it.

Tall and headstrong, Eliza expects to remain an "unclaimed treasure." Devastated in the wake of the Civil War, she leaves her home in Texas and sets out for New Mexico's Sangre de Cristo mountains in search of peace and new purpose but discovers a wild western frontier where former enemies—Yankees and Rebels, Freedmen and Indians—square off in the quest for land and gold.

Eliza must confront her prejudices and fears, and Jacob Craig embodies that conflict. The mountain man wins her trust with his gentle strength, but he harbors a secret. As a Union sharp-shooter, he met her fiancé on the field of battle and cost him his life. Can she forgive him? To find peace and the future she yearns for, Eliza must first find in God a faith more precious than gold.

A real ghost town comes to life in this award-winning story of love, forgiveness, and the sovereignty of God. Christian historical fiction readers will love the way this story combines the adventure of classic historical western fiction with a dash of romance.


## Home Sweet Hole: A Folio of "Feasible Fantasy" Floor Plans

"In a hole in the ground there lived a Hobbit..." but Hobbits aren't the only ones with down-to-earth dreams. This folio of "feasible fantasy" floor plans gives you a fun-loving peek inside a dozen earth-bermed dwellings in an imaginary borough of burrows—all drawn to scale as if the builder, himself, were offering an open house tour.  Also available in paperback.

*9780692547762*